STOUR VALLEY WALK

GW01495679

Discover the many faces of Kent

ACKNOWLEDGEMENT

We are grateful to the Stour Valley Society for their assistance in the development of the Stour Valley Walk and in the preparation of this guidebook.

The Stour Valley Society was formed in 1969 to seek to preserve the beauty of the valley, to be watchful of all happenings which might threaten that beauty, and to foster its quiet enjoyment by the public. The society has always believed that the most rewarding way to do this is on foot along the public footpaths which traverse the valley. In 1974-83 it published a series of walk maps, prepared by the Rev. Christopher Donaldson, one of the society's founders, to cover the valley between the source at Lenham and Canterbury. Subsequently in 1985 Mr Donaldson authored a book of walks in the lower valley below Canterbury.

The Stour Valley Walk, promoted by Kent County Council with the collaboration of the society is a linear walk along the valley between Ashford and Sandwich which, for the most part, follows the routes of the earlier publications.

Anyone interested in joining the society may contact the membership secretary, currently Mr John Nunn, 2a The Foreland, Canterbury CT1 3NT, telephone Canterbury 453724

Designed by Kent County Council Public Relations Unit

Text by Geoffrey Allanson, Christopher Donaldson, Robert Lloyd and Kenneth Snelson

Photographs by Andy Wickham

Maps by Kent County Council, County Visuals

Typesetting by Copperfields, 1 Bramley Road, East Peckham, Tonbridge, Kent TN12 5BN

Printed in Great Britain by Alcris Ltd, Unit 4, Chapel Park, Church Road Business Centre, Murston, Sittingbourne, Kent ME10 3RS

Published by Kent County Council, Planning Department, Springfield, Maidstone, Kent ME14 2LX, with assistance from the Countryside Commission.

First published September 1990

Copyright © 1990 Kent County Council

All rights reserved. No part of this publication may be reproduced in any way without the written permission of the publishers.

ISBN 1 873010 02 8

Front cover: Crundale
Back cover: Great Stour River at Longport Bridge, Willesborough Lees

The design of the Stour Valley Walk logo is based on the head of the grey heron.

It is one of the best known and easily recognised birds – a patient, silent, almost motionless hunter of eels and other fish, frogs, even small mammals. It is usually seen near rivers, lakes and ponds and in winter, on the seashore.

Herons are mainly 'resident' in their established tree top nesting colonies, which they occupy from February to September. However, some birds do 'migrate' to and from the continent.

The national population is thought to be some 5000 pairs with the largest known colony found in Kent at the Northwood Hill RSPB Reserve at High Halstow. Of the 250 or so pairs found in Kent, up to 200 are found at Northwood Hill.

The oldest known colony in Britain is at Chilham, but the size of the colony has declined from more than 100 pairs in 1957 to less than 10 in recent years. As well as the colony at Chilham there are a number of other small colonies found along the River Stour. The river is frequently visited by herons throughout the year in their search for food and the heron is very much a bird of the Stour Valley.

Chilham Castle

WALKING ADVICE

No season of the year is closed to walkers; enjoyment can be gained from walking on a bright crisp winter's morning, or on an Indian summer's day in the autumn. Equally rewarding is a springtime walk when the countryside is full of new life and growth.

Be prepared for cold and wet weather. Take with you clothes which are warm and waterproof. Sections of the path may be muddy after periods of rain so wear strong comfortable and, waterproof footwear. Inexpensive overtrousers will protect you from any discomfort caused by walking through high vegetation after rain. In case you come across a path which has become overgrown, you would find it useful to carry secateurs to help clear the way. Take care when crossing major roads, particularly the A28 at Milton Bridge and Stodmarsh Road.

Reckon on walking 2 or 2½ miles an hour. However, the distances and time for the walk are shown on the route maps, and in the information. Allow more time if it has been wet, if you are elderly or have children or inexperienced walkers with you.

The route has been established in conjunction with landowners and follows public rights of way.

Please remember that most of the public paths cross private land. You are walking through a place of work; enjoy the countryside but please show respect and consideration for its life and work.

Remember to leave things as they are – fasten all gates and take your litter home with you otherwise it can injure people and animals (including wildlife). Guard against all risk of fire, especially in dry weather.

Dogs should be under control at all times, if not on a lead they can run surprisingly long distances in a short time and cause distress to people and animals not in the immediate vicinity and therefore out of sight of the owner.

Footpaths are for people on foot only, remember to always to use gates and stiles to cross fences and hedges. If the path goes through a growing crop please walk in single file. Paths were mostly developed as routes from farms to the nearest village and so were not designed for large numbers of walkers. If you are in a large party of walkers, landowners would consider it a courtesy to receive warning, particularly if the party goes through a farmyard.

Please leave wild flowers for others to enjoy. Remember that crops and animals are the farmers livelihood so please leave them alone.

Sandwich Quay

To the best of our knowledge the historical content and other information is believed to be correct. We would be grateful if you would inform us of any changes, omissions or errors, so that modifications can be made in subsequent revisions of the book.

USING THE GUIDEBOOK

Although it is possible to walk the route of the Stour Valley Walk in either direction the maps have been arranged in sequence, in eight convenient sections, from Ashford to Sandwich. The location map alongside shows how the route lies in relation to each section. Each section in the book corresponds to the colour on this map.

DISTANCES AND TIME

The distances and times for each section of the walk are shown on the map spreads or in the information below.

ROUTE MAP INFORMATION

The route maps are reproduced from the Ordnance Survey maps with the sanction of the controller of HM Stationery Office; Crown copyright reserved.

The maps are aligned north/south on each page. The scale appears on each map spread.

MAPS

Ordnance Survey map sheet numbers and titles

Landranger Series, scale 1:50,000-1¼" to the mile
189 Ashford and Romney Marsh area
179 Canterbury and East Kent area

Pathfinder Series, scale 1:25,000-2½" to the mile
TR 04/14 Ashford and Lyminge
TR 05/15 Canterbury and Chilham
TR 26/36 Margate and St Nicholas at Wade
TR 25/35 Sandwich and Deal

Preston Valley Grove

PLANNING A WALK

This walk has been developed with regard to the good rail and road communications which will enable you to return conveniently to your starting point.

The route is 38 miles in length and can be undertaken as a long distance walk over two or three days, perhaps a weekend. Ashford, Canterbury and Sandwich are all easily reached by train from London and most parts of Kent, Surrey and East Sussex, via Faversham or Ashford.

If you wish to undertake the Stour Valley Walk in sections you need to be aware of problems of returning to your starting point. Possible solutions might be as follows:
a) using two cars, one at the starting point and the other at the proposed finishing point.
b) using one car and public transport. If relying on infrequent bus services it is suggested that you make your outward journey by bus thus returning confidently to your car or base.
c) retracing your steps – the scenery can look surprisingly different when you are walking the other way.

The walk can be undertaken in sections as follows:

Ashford – Wye: 6 miles, allow 3 hours
Wye – Godmersham: 5½ miles, allow 2½ hours
Godmersham – Chilham: 4½ miles, allow 2¼ hours
Chilham – Chartham: 3¾ miles, allow 1¾ hours
Chartham – Canterbury: 5 miles, allow 2½ hours
Canterbury – Sturry: 3½ miles, allow 1¾ hours
Sturry – Upstreet: 6½ miles, allow 3¼ hours
Upstreet – East Stourmouth: 3 miles, allow 1½ hours
East Stourmouth – Sandwich: 7½ miles, allow 3¾ hours

Access for each of the above places is as follows:

Ashford – bus and train
Wye – bus and train
Godmersham – bus only
Chilham – bus and train
Chartham – bus and train
Canterbury – bus and train
Sturry – bus and train
Upstreet – bus only
East Stourmouth – bus only (infrequent)
Sandwich – bus and train

TRANSPORT

Car Parking
Car parking places are shown on the route maps. Please note that these are not necessarily car parks. If a car park is not available please park thoughtfully and sensibly to avoid causing an obstruction or damaging roadside verges.

Bus Services
Most local bus services are provided by East Kent Buses. Route numbers are shown on the route maps. For details of services please telephone the following enquiry offices:
Ashford (0233) 20342/20344
Canterbury (0227) 472082
Sandwich (0304) 612067

Other services provided by:
Poynters of Wye – services 667 668 669 (0233) 812002
Postbus services (0227) 475299

Train Services
The following British Rail stations provide access to the Stour Valley Walk. For details of services (Table 207 in the BR timetable) please telephone the information office as follows:
for Ashford, Wye, Chilham, Chartham, Canterbury West, Sturry and Sandwich, tel: Canterbury (0277) 45441

Coach Services
Coach services operate from London (Victoria Coach Station) to Ashford, Canterbury and Sandwich. The number of daily services each way are 4, 9 and 1 respectively. Telephone enquiries: London 071-730 0202 or Thanet (0843) 581333

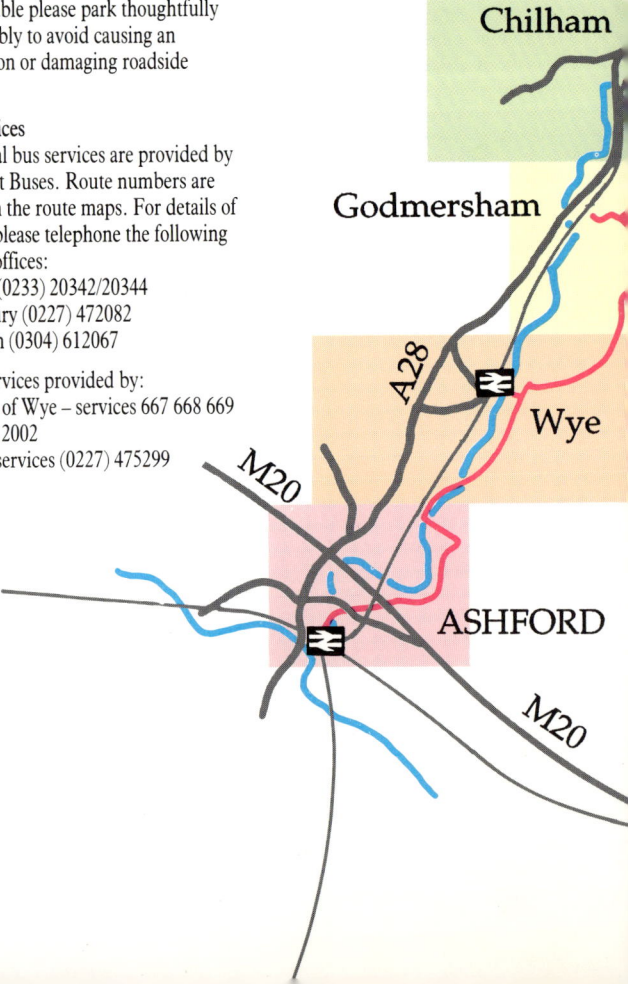

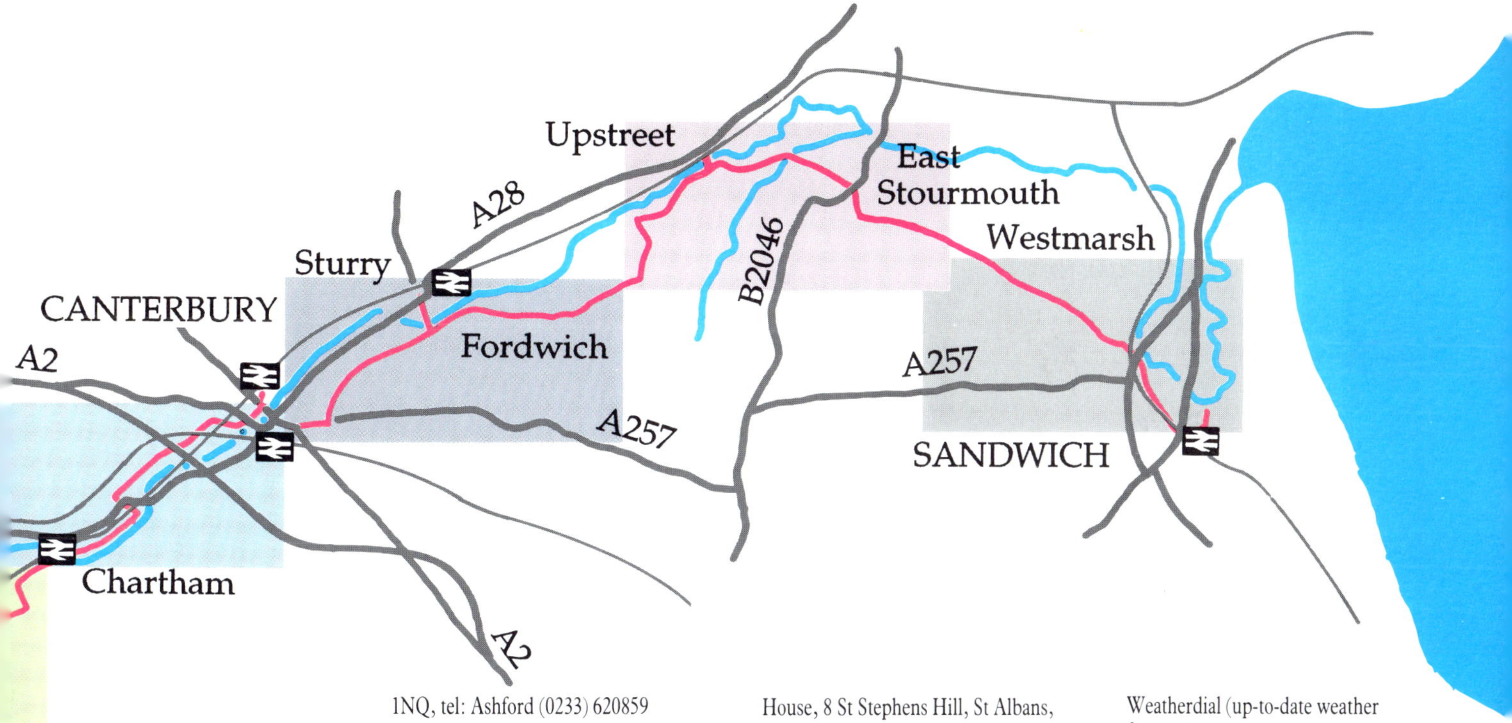

ACCOMMODATION

Bed and Breakfast establishments are located in the following places:
Ashford, Wye, Chilham (1 mile), Chartham, Canterbury, Fordwich, Wickhambreaux (1¼ miles), Upstreet (½ mile), East Stourmouth, Ash (1½ miles), and Sandwich.

Please telephone one of the tourist information centres, listed elsewhere, for details.

The Ramblers Association (also listed) publishes the Ramblers Year Book which contains an accommodation list.

Camp sites located near the route:

Ashford (3 miles): Broadhembury Farm Caravan and Camping Park, Steeds Lane, Kingsnorth, Ashford TN26 1NQ, tel: Ashford (0233) 620859

Canterbury (1 mile): St Martins Touring Caravan and Camping Park, Bekesbourne Lane, Canterbury, Kent, tel: Canterbury (0227) 463216

Sandwich (¼ mile): Sandwich Leisure Park, Woodnesborough Road, Sandwich, Kent CT13 0AA, tel: Sandwich (0304) 612681

Youth Hostel: Canterbury (½ mile)

'Ellerslie', 54 New Dover Road, Canterbury, Kent CT1 3DT, tel: Canterbury (0227) 462911

Details of membership can be obtained from YHA National Office, Trevelyan House, 8 St Stephens Hill, St Albans, Herts AL1 2DY, tel: St Albans (0727) 55215. You may join the YHA on arrival at the hostel, but prior booking is advisable.

USEFUL ADDRESSES AND/OR TELEPHONE NUMBERS

If you have any comments or suggestions about this or any other recreational route please contact:

Recreation Paths Officer, Planning Department, Kent County Council, Springfield, Maidstone, Kent ME14 2LX. tel: Maidstone (0622) 696168

The routes should not be obstructed in any way, but if they are please contact the district footpaths officers as follows:

between Ashford and Mystole – Ashford Borough Council, tel: Asford (0233) 637311 ext 341
between Mystole and Grove Ferry – Canterbury City Council, tel: Canterbury (0277) 763763 ext 4834
between Grove Ferry and Sandwich – Dover District Council, tel: Dover (0304) 821199 ext 5398

Weatherdial (up-to-date weather forecast)
Inland Kent 0898 14 12 12
Margate and Thames Estuary 0898 14 12 13

Tourist Information (including accommodation lists)

Ashford: Tourist Information Centre, Lower High Street, Ashford, Kent TN24 8TE, tel: Ashford (0233) 37311 ext 316

Canterbury: Visitor Information Centre, 34 St Margarets Street, Canterbury, Kent CT1 2TG, tel: Canterbury (0227) 766567

Sandwich: Tourist Information Centre, Guildhall, Sandwich, Kent CT13 9AH, tel: Sandwich (0304) 613565

If having undertaken this Walk, you find that walking really appeals to you, you may wish to consider joining The Ramblers, in which case please contact: The Ramblers Association, 1/5 Wandsworth Road, London SW8 2XX, tel: 071-582 6878

Sandwich Bay

Pledge's Mill, Ashford

SIGNING AND WAYMARKING

The Stour Valley Walk logo and waymarks are used to show the line of the route; you will see them fixed to waymark posts, poles or the posts of gates or stiles. The Walk has been waymarked in such a way that it is possible for you to walk the route in either direction.

At regular points along the route you will see metal signs fixed to lamp posts or some other post. These show access to the route from railway stations and/or bus routes, and display the logo and arrow coloured brown and white. The wording 'Stour Valley Walk' will also be found on the special cast signs in Canterbury.

These access points will enable you to devise your own shorter walks utilising public transport.

Stour Valley Logo
(green and black logo on white disc)

Linear Waymark
(yellow arrow on black disc)

Stour Valley Walk Sign
(brown and white)

KEY TO MAP SYMBOLS

——	Stour Valley Walk – fully signed and waymarked		Public house
- - -	Spur (access point) – fully signed and waymarked		Pub food
....	Optional detour		Cafe/restaurant
101	Feature of interest		Picnic site
13	Miles from Ashford		Foodstore
	Railway station		View point
	Bus route		Seat
P	Car parking	HWM	High water mark
	Telephone		Caution – take care
i	Tourist Information		English Heritage property
WC	Toilet		North Downs Way
	Accommodation		Saxon Shore Way
▲	Camp site		Centenary Walks
	Youth hostel		Wantsum Walks
			Circular Walk

1

Ashford – Grid reference TR035448, 3½ miles, allow 1⅓ hours

Ashford

Ashford was formerly a Wealden market town, located at the crossing of roads from Maidstone to Hythe and from Rye to Canterbury and where the Great Stour could be forded. It became more important with the coming of the South Eastern Railway in 1842 and developed both as a junction (the branch to Canterbury opened in 1896) and a railway town with engine works which opened in 1847. It is destined to become Britain's first international railway station on the line from France through the Channel Tunnel.

St Mary's Church, Ashford

The walk begins and ends at the Stour Centre (2) in Tannery Lane. Adjacent to the Borough Council Offices, the centre caters for recreation and sport; both are situated between the Great Stour and the East Stour. The river nearer the Station Road is man-made and was

Lenham Pond, source of Great Stour

Stour Valley Flood Plain

From the footbridge over the M20 (the main road to the Channel Tunnel) you can see over the two Unilever factories (one makes soup, the other makes and packages perfumes and flavours). Between the outskirts of Ashford and Wye the route follows the flat valley through which the Great Stour meanders in its flood plain towards the North Downs. As you cross mainly hedgeless arable 'prairie' farmlands, the downs dominate the skyline to the north.

As you walk along Blackwall Road you will see to the west the gravel workings of Conningbrook Quarry (4). Much of the gravel dates back to the last inter-glacial period and was deposited in a river bed cut some 15 feet below the present surface when the sea level was lower. Remains of mammoth and woolly rhinoceros have been found. There are several workings between Ashford and Canterbury. Various restoration plans will be implemented when the gravel has been dug out – filling and reinstatement to agriculture or left as landscaped lakes.

known as the Lord's Cut since the Lord of the Manor made this to improve his milling operations at the mill (3) at the bottom of East Hill.

FEATURES OF INTEREST

1 **St Mary's Church, Ashford**
   15th-century cruciform church with magnificent central tower.

2 **Stour Centre**
   The Stour Centre, adjacent to Ashford Borough Council Offices, is a multi-purpose sports and recreation complex.

3 **Pledge's Mill**
   Once an operating water mill, the wheel of which is an interesting industrial relic.

4 **Conningbrook Quarry**
   Gravel extracted from these workings dates back to the last inter-glacial period.

Blackwall Farm, Hinxhill Parish

2

Grid reference TRO35448 – Warren Wood, 4 miles, allow 1½ hours

The path crosses the river twice; this takes water from Ashford's sewage treatment plant and has little fish life at this stage. In the tributary streams which join it to the north, particularly those from the east, the water is clearer and large pike lurk there. There are birds – some swans on the river and, when it overflows, geese and herons. It is lower down that the river becomes a unique chalk stream when it receives spring water from the aquifer beneath the downs.

North Downs Scarp

To the north, across the river, can be seen Boughton Aluph Church (5) which used to provide a resting place for pilgrims on their way to Canterbury. To the north-east, on Wye Downs, 'The Junipers', a plantation sorely ravaged in the 1987 hurricane, was planted to commemorate victory in the Napoleonic Wars, then Wye's 'Crown' (6) cut out in the chalk hillside by Wye College students to record the coronation of Edward VII in 1902. Further to the east, is the Nature Conservancy Council's National Nature Reserve; over 100 hectares in extent lying on the steep face of the escarpment and an unspoiled remnant of the rolling chalk downlands of southern England once famed for their fauna and flora, expecially orchids and butterflies.

Wye

The town of Wye commands the river gap through the downs; we see white painted gables of the dormitory estate backed by the squat-towered church. Once it had a tall spire but that was struck by lightening in 1572. Wye is a very old settlement, important before recorded history, lived in by Romans, Saxons, Normans and still important as an internationally renowned centre for agricultural learning and research. The route passes through much of the heritage centre, joining Bridge Street as it rises from the seventeenth century bridge (built on the site of the ford where the ancient North Downs trackway crossed the Stour), the Domesday-recorded water mill and the Victorian railway station.

Bridge Street and Church Street

Swan House (134-140 Bridge Street) is passed, with its late Norman foundations; most of the structure however is 16th century. The modern house next to the Methodist Chapel has a Norman undercroft. Church Street has fifteenth and sixteenth century houses with Georgian and Victorian facades. The street once had at least five inns; now only one remains. The street is dominated by the Church of St Martin and St Gregory (7), which was built in the late 12th century when the former royal manor was in the possession of the Abbots of Battle. It was considerably modified by Kempe in the mid 15th century and again at the beginning of the 18th century following the 1685 collapse of the tower which shattered the long chancel and both transepts. The rebuilding was to a reduced size – no transepts, only a short apse, and the present stubby tower.

Wye College

To the right of the church is Wye College (8), the oldest quadrangle of which dates back to Kempe's foundation in 1432. Wye is Britain's smallest university town – a mini Oxbridge – and the happy presence of youny people, many from overseas, gives the town a particular personality. The history of Wye College is long and interesting. Originally founded as a secular establishment for priests, it was used during the centuries following the dissolution as a grammar school, private residence and village school. In 1894 it was purchased for conversion into the South Eastern Agricultural College, and was recognised as an institution by the University of London in 1900 and incorporated by Royal Charter in 1948. To the east is passed the College research greenhouses where varied experiments are carried out. To the south-east you can glimpse Coldharbour Farm where one of Wye College's new ventures is located – the Countryside Management Centre.

Tomb, Wye churchyard

North Downs

North of Wye are the undulating ridges and dry valleys of the North Downs, officially designated an area of outstanding natural beauty (AONB). The valleys were formed at the end of the last ice age when they were gouged out by solifluction and running water from melting ice and snow when permafrost made the ground impermeable. Now they are the gathering grounds through which rainwater percolates to the underlying chalk aquifer which serves as the reservoir supplying water to Ashford and Canterbury.

The southernmost valley is the natural amphitheatre of Fanscombe (9) where one George Kennet of Amage ran annual horse races before large

Church of St Martin and St Gregory, Wye

enthusiastic crowds for some 40 years from the early 1840s after which the race course moved to Wye. To the north-west is Olantigh House (10), its grounds devastated by the October 1987 hurricane, now replanted to begin the long road to parkland maturity. There have been a succession of mansions on the Olantigh site and some famous families lived there. Cardinal Kempe, who founded Wye College, was born there in 1380. Another less illustrious resident was a perpetrator of the 'South Sea Bubble'.

Marriage Farm (11), due east of the 'Ash' by which the route passes, is a corruption of the old English 'moere hryeg' meaning boundary ridge and still lies at the boundary between Wye and Crundale parishes.

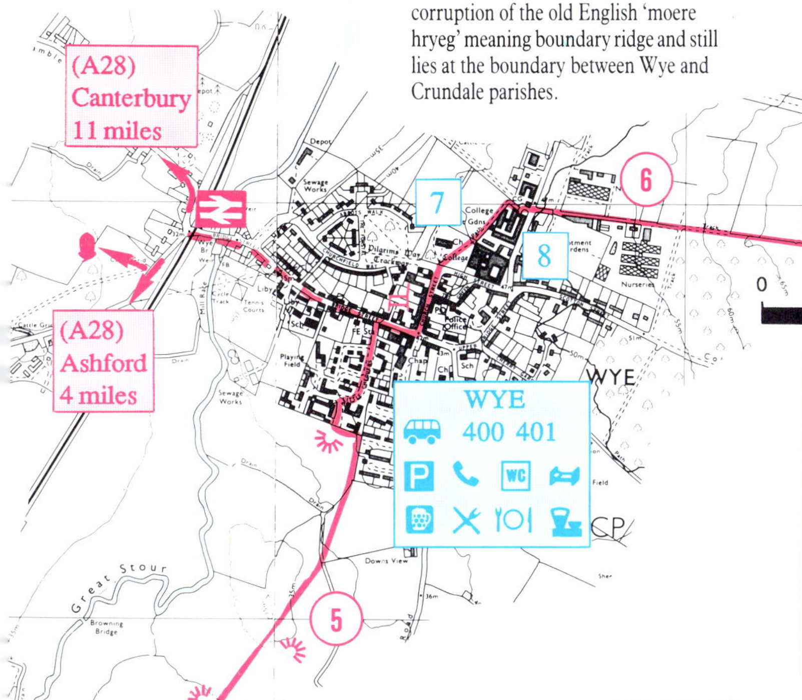

Wye Downs

Church Street, Wye, from Wye church

FEATURES OF INTEREST

5 All Saints Church, Boughton Aluph
A large cruciform church built mainly in the 13th and late 14th centuries.

6 Wye's 'Crown'
Cut out in the chalk downs to record the coronation of Edward VII in 1902.

7 Church of St Martin and St Gregory, Wye
Built in the 12th century, the church was modified in the early 18th century following the collapse of the tower in 1685.

8 Wye College
The college, founded by Cardinal Kempe in 1432 is now the agricultural school of the University of London.

9 Fanscombe
A natural amphitheatre in the chalk downs where George Kennet of Amaghe ran annual horse races in the early 19th century.

10 Olantigh House
An 18th century building on the site of the original home of Cardinal Kempe, and his birthplace in 1380.

11 Marriage Farm
The name is a corruption of the old English 'moere hryeg' meaning boundary ridge.

3

Warren Wood – Grid reference TR089515, 3½ miles, allow 1½ hours

Crundale

Crundale village is now distanced from its 12th-14th century church (13) facing across the dry valley. Crundale House (12) incorporates the timber frame of an early 13th century Wealden house. Note also the land cleared for extending the lime works to the north-east of the village; an extensive Roman settlement was on this site.

The route leads a little west of Eggarton Manor along the broad dry valley between Crundale and Godmersham, its chalk enriched by windblown brickearth deposited at the close of the Ice Age. This is an ancient landscape.

Godmersham

Though the surviving round barrows are on the less hospitable gravels and clay with flints, prehistoric field systems can be seen on the grass slopes of the downs above and west of Godmersham. Earth banks, due to soil slippage and cultivation indicate field boundaries that extended along the slope under nearby woodland and present-day arable land. To the west towards Bilting are the remains of a three-field system.

The chalk valley itself is still farmed by the manors mentioned in the Anglo Saxon Charter of 824 AD. Even the boundaries of Godmersham Parish have remained almost unchanged for 1000 years. The building at Court Lodge (15), Godmersham, like its Chartham counterpart, was started by the church around 1270, to help feed the monks at Christ Church Priory, Canterbury, only to be wantonly destroyed in 1955.

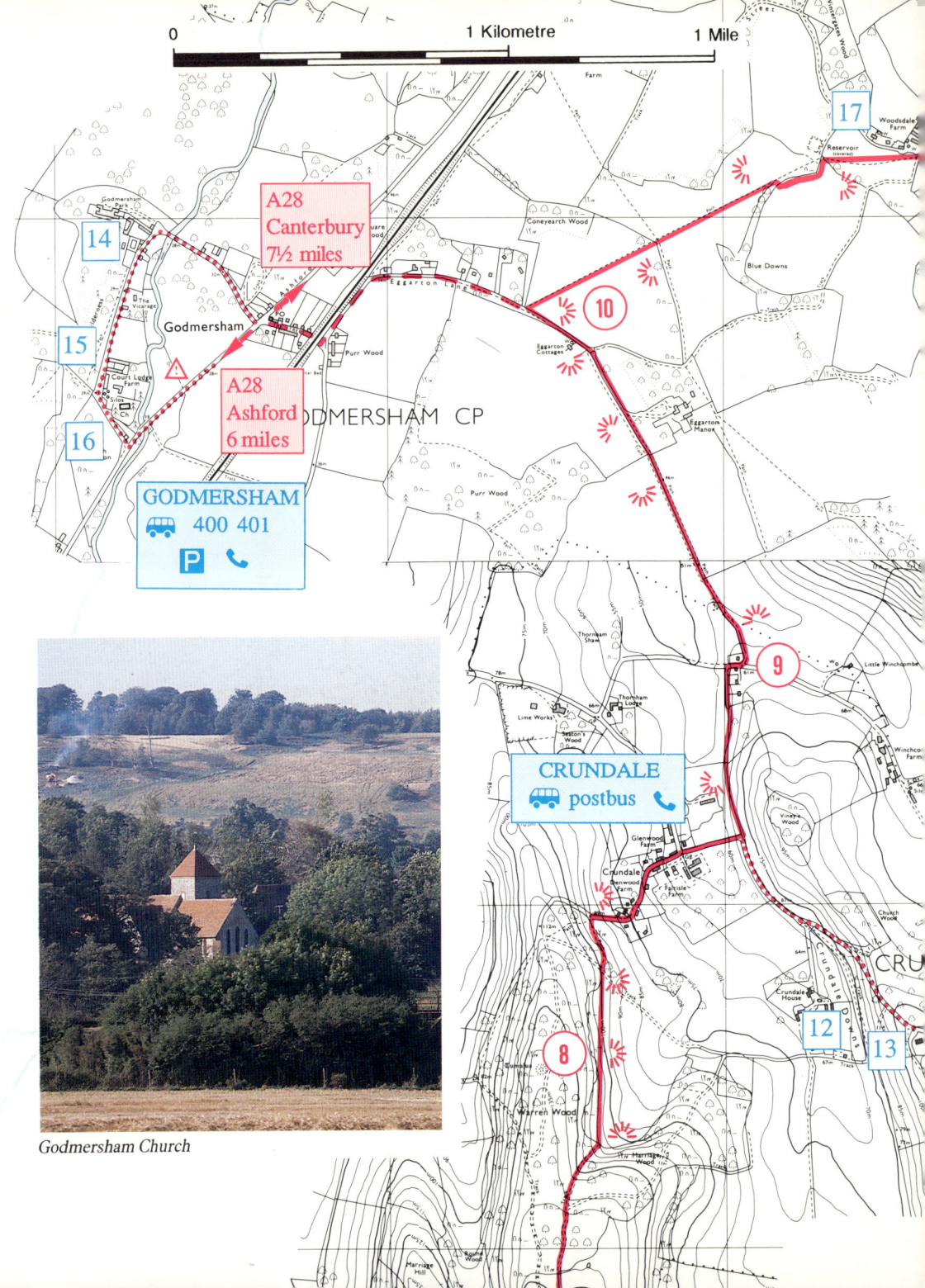

Godmersham Church

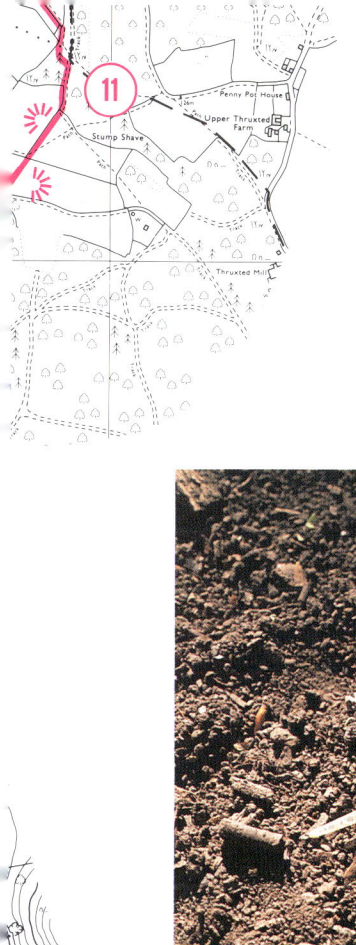

Michaelmas daisy

Woodland floor, Crundale

FEATURES OF INTEREST

12 Crundale House
The house incorporates the timber frame of an early 13th-century Wealden house.

13 St Mary's Church, Crundale
The 12th to 14th-century church has an incised slab to a 15th-century vicar. Much restored.

14 Godmersham Park
The house, rebuilt in 1935, is Georgian and belonged to Edward Knight, whose sister, Jane Austen was a frequent visitor here.

15 Court Lodge Farm, Godmersham
Court Lodge which was built c1270 to help feed the monks at Christ Church Priory, Canterbury, was destroyed in 1955.

16 Church of St Lawrence the Martyr, Godmersham
A heavily restored church with a Norman tower and 13th-century chancel; also a 12th-century bas-relief of St Thomas Becket.

17 Woodsdale Farm
Pottery was made here in former times, in kilns fired by wood from Denge Wood above.

Godmersham Park

Godmersham Park (14) is an early Georgian house incorporating Ford Manor but largely rebuilt in 1835. Jane Austen was a frequent visitor when the house belonged to her brother Edward Knight and in all probability drew much material for 'Mansfield Park' and 'Pride and Prejudice' from her visits. The upper part of the park, also badly damaged by the 1987 hurricane, is traversed by the Pilgrim's Way before it enters Chilham Park. In the valley the turnpike road came through in 1834, replacing the old road that kept to the western bank on its way through Mountain Street to Chilham.

Note the depth of the valley which the Great Stour has cut through the chalk since the Alpine movements some 20-30 million years ago. This is an area of springs. The river becomes clear and cool. Now it is the classic chalk stream and a home for trout.

The route passes Woodsdale Farm (17) where pottery was made in former times, in kilns fired by wood from the Denge Wood above.

4

Grid reference TR089515 – Shalmsford Street, 4 miles, allow 1½ hours

Along this stretch of the walk the wood is encroaching on cleared pasture as it does periodically when agriculture is less prosperous. Traditionally, rape is grown after cereal crops are harvested in order to fatten lambs from Kent sheep after grass loses its feed value.

To the east of Chilham the route follows the old carriage road (18) above the river along which Jane Austen must have travelled when visiting the Fagg family ("I never saw so plain a family") at "so pretty" Mystole in 1813.

Chilham

Across the Great Stour is Chilham at the end of a steep-sided ridge, thickly screened by trees. Its fine church (21) and square of half-timbered houses make it one of the prettiest villages in Kent. At its western edge is Chilham Castle (22), a Jacobean mansion of 1616, allegedly to an Inigo Jones design. Nearby, can be seen the octagonal 12th century keep of its predecessor, protected by a 14th century curtain wall and a fore-building on the foundations of an 11th century castle which itself occupied the site of Roman fortifications. Below, the gardens were designed by Capability Brown in 1771. At the foot of the ridge, and within Chilham Park between the castle and the old Ashford Road (23) is the heronry which inspired the symbol for the Stour Valley Walk. It dates back at least 800 years.

Jullieberrie's Grave

Jullieberrie's Grave, (19) a Neolithic long barrow, may be some 5,000 years

Chilham Water Mill

old and is one of the few to be found in east Kent.

Chilham Water Mill

Chilham Water Mill (20), splendidly restored and in the possession of the Mid Kent Water Company, is one of the best sights of the valley, standing proudly over its mill pool with the river on one side and the lake on the other. There is a long history of mills on this site going back to the Domesday Book including a 'French Mill', part of Henry VIII's Chilham Estate. The present structure was erected between 1830 and 1850 and is a timber-framed building of five storeys. Inside it has great posts of oak, six in number and eight inches square, which rise the whole height of the mill and support much of the weight. At a later date a steam boiler and engine were added to keep operations going when there was a flow of water, but these were not used after 1927 and by 1934 the first part of the mill's working life had come to an end. No attention was given thereafter to the mill until its rescue by purchase by the Mid Kent Water Company in 1960. The whole of this charming site (including the lovely mill house) has been restored and reflects the greatest credit on the Company.

Chilham Lake

The lake (24) is also owned by the Company. It is the first and most beautiful of the various sheets of water created by gravel digging and which are to be found close to the river between Chilham and Grove Ferry. For the lakeside walk binoculars are needed, for many birds come here; coot, Canada geese, black headed gull, mallard, pochard and tufted duck in abundance. (If towards evening, look out for the cormorants going to roost in a tree two thirds of the way along the lake). As a rule, a heron is to be seen and one or two great crested grebes, a bird which faced extinction at one time when its feathers were sought for the hats of Edwardian ladies, but which (especially in the last 40 years) has re-established itself. If one is fortunate, the glorious colours of a Kingfisher may flash past. A pair of mute swans invariably raise their young on the lake and another pair do so on the nearby river. One of the fascinations for the regular visitor is to watch the progress of the cygnets. Rarer birds, especially in late winter, are red-crested pochards, goosanders, ruddy duck (an American import, fairly numerous in the west of England) and gadwall, one of the dullest plumaged of British ducks. The plant life too is rich and varied with specially fine groups of bulrush and yellow flag. Whatever the time of year there is peace and serenity about Chilham Lake, despite the railway and busy main road being so near.

Mystole

A mile above the lake along the route is Mystole (25) another of the great country houses of the valley. It was built in the early 18th century, but was considerably altered and added to by the eminent architect, Sir Reginald Blomfield, at the turn of the present century. The Fagg family, and later the Pomfrets lived here for many years, but since the Second World War the whole place has been turned into flats, and the various cottages are now all privately owned.

Chilham village square

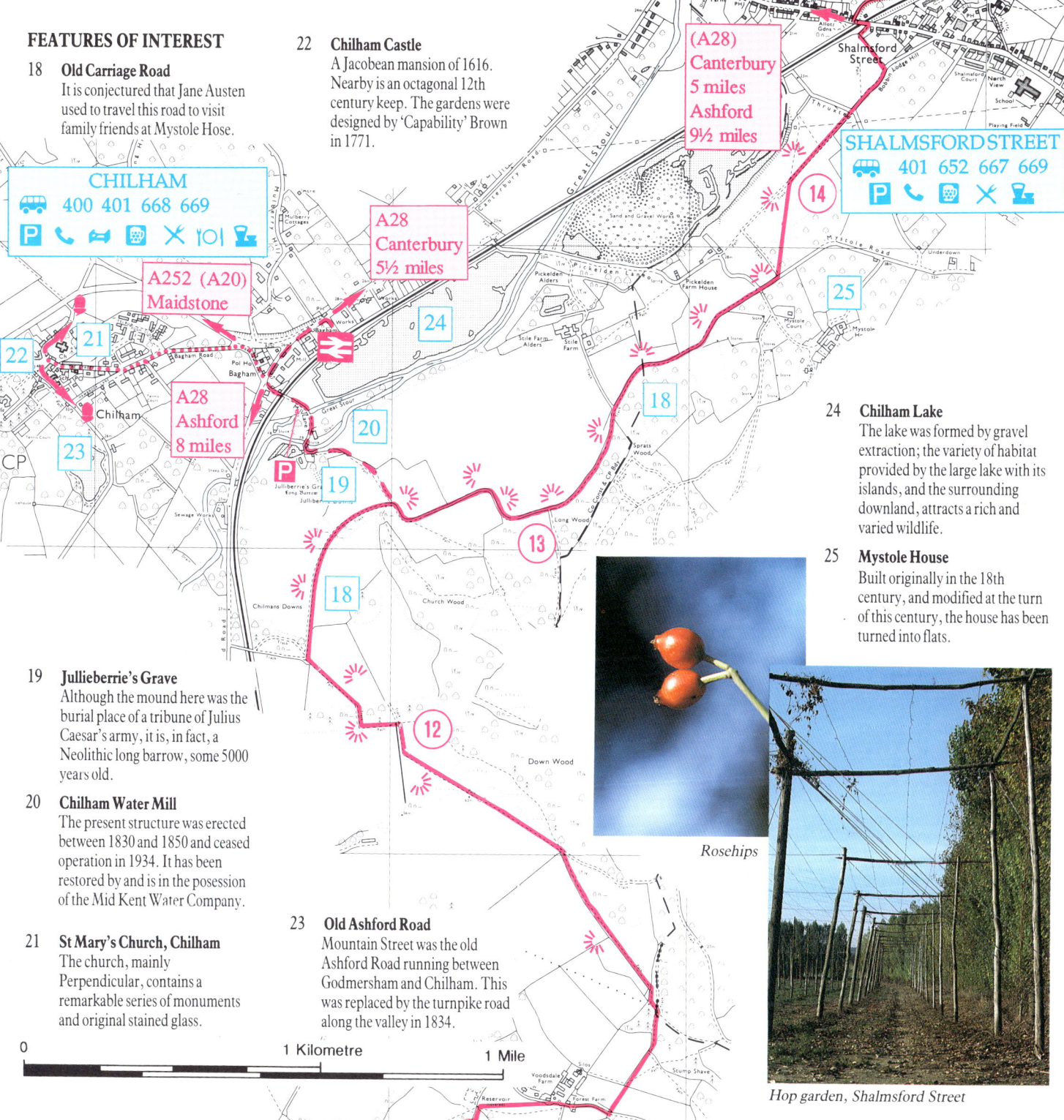

FEATURES OF INTEREST

18 Old Carriage Road
It is conjectured that Jane Austen used to travel this road to visit family friends at Mystole House.

19 Jullieberrie's Grave
Although the mound here was the burial place of a tribune of Julius Caesar's army, it is, in fact, a Neolithic long barrow, some 5000 years old.

20 Chilham Water Mill
The present structure was erected between 1830 and 1850 and ceased operation in 1934. It has been restored by and is in the posession of the Mid Kent Water Company.

21 St Mary's Church, Chilham
The church, mainly Perpendicular, contains a remarkable series of monuments and original stained glass.

22 Chilham Castle
A Jacobean mansion of 1616. Nearby is an octagonal 12th century keep. The gardens were designed by 'Capability' Brown in 1771.

23 Old Ashford Road
Mountain Street was the old Ashford Road running between Godmersham and Chilham. This was replaced by the turnpike road along the valley in 1834.

24 Chilham Lake
The lake was formed by gravel extraction; the variety of habitat provided by the large lake with its islands, and the surrounding downland, attracts a rich and varied wildlife.

25 Mystole House
Built originally in the 18th century, and modified at the turn of this century, the house has been turned into flats.

Rosehips

Hop garden, Shalmsford Street

Chartham – Canterbury, 5½ miles, allow 2¼ hours

Chartham

Between Shalmsford Street and Chartham lies Deanery Farm (26), possessed by the Deans of Canterbury until the 17th century. An 18th century front masks an earlier house. The water meadows which stretch from the house to the river have, in recent years, been a planning battleground between would-be gravel diggers and the large proportion of local residents who wish to keep these activities away from the village and the meadows. The villagers lost and a fourteen year programme of extraction and restoration is in prospect.

At Chartham Green, notice especially an ancient half-timbered hall house on the north side, and De l'Angle House (27) in the corner, built at the turn of the 18th century, has a bust of King Charles II surveying the passing scene.

The main interest here lies in the church (28), though the churchyard has been spoiled by having all the tombstones placed around the wall like naughty children in order that the mowing may be easier. This was a practice given the seal of approval in several churchyards in the 1950's but it is now generally recognised that the character of the place is thus taken away.

However, the mainly 14th-century church is one of the best in the neighbourhood. There is a good roof, with a fine 'scissors' effect at the central crossing and large boss to cover the joint. The windows, four on each side of the chancel are built with the star effect of 'Kentish Tracery' and at the head of the 'stars' of the western pairs (nearest the screen) is some 14th-century glass.

Apple Blossom

The south transept is the home of a large monument by the great (resident) Flemish sculptor Michael Rzsbrack, 1751, to Sarah Young (née Fagg) and her husband Sir William Young. The monument contains two of Rzsbrack's favourite devices. His subjects are in Roman attire and a putto (the small angelic figure) extinguishes the torch of life. As usual the inscription is lengthy but worth reading. Rzsbrack died in 1770 at the age of 76 and no doubt a rich man. He still has around 200 monuments or pieces of sculpture in England, fifteen in Westminster Abbey alone.

Chartham Church's fame, however, rests upon its quartet of brasses, with the supreme effigy of Sir William de Septvans, 1306. Notice the absence of a helmet, the 'vans' (used for drying corn) and the crossed legs, once taken to mean a crusader, but a myth now exploded.

Chartham Paper Mill (29), nearby, is stark and foreboding. This industrial complex (there has been a mill here for over 250 years) is a strange place to find in a Kentish village, but it is a provider of much local employment and a reminder that the various users of the valley have to co-exist with and respect one another.

Cricket is played on the large ground near the church at weekends, and on a fine summer day the game with the church in the background is indeed a pleasant sight. Above the village on the downs are the buildings of St Augustine's Hospital, a better name than that previously used, Chartham Asylum, but along with other such institutions it is now being run down and closure imminent.

The route follows the river bank between Milton and Chartham, indeed it would be hard to stray as most of the fields have been dug up for gravel, though restoration is promised and in the area near Milton Bridge has already taken place. In this area the river is a true chalk stream. There are trout here in some number and salmon have been found as far up as this too.

Horton and Milton Chapels

On the opposite bank two small former chapels are passed, Horton (30) and Milton (31). Horton, which is recorded as being in existence in 1380, has been used as a barn for the past 250 years, but Milton, no doubt because it was still used as a church, was totally restored and renewed by the Victorians. It was closed for worship only in the 1970's, and now stands somewhat forlorn among huge heaps of gravel and machinery.

Howfield and Tonford Manors

Near the A28 (Ashford-Canterbury road) is an important house (32), successively Howfield Farm, Manor and now Hotel with a 17th-century brick north front, but concealing work of the 13th century. Further along the track is Tonford Manor (34), one of the best moderate sized houses in the neighbourhood, dating from the mid-15th century, and known in the mid-20th century as the home of playwright Christopher Hassall. To the east lie the outskirts of Canterbury, Thanington Without (outside the city walls), but all this is overwhelmed by the view of the

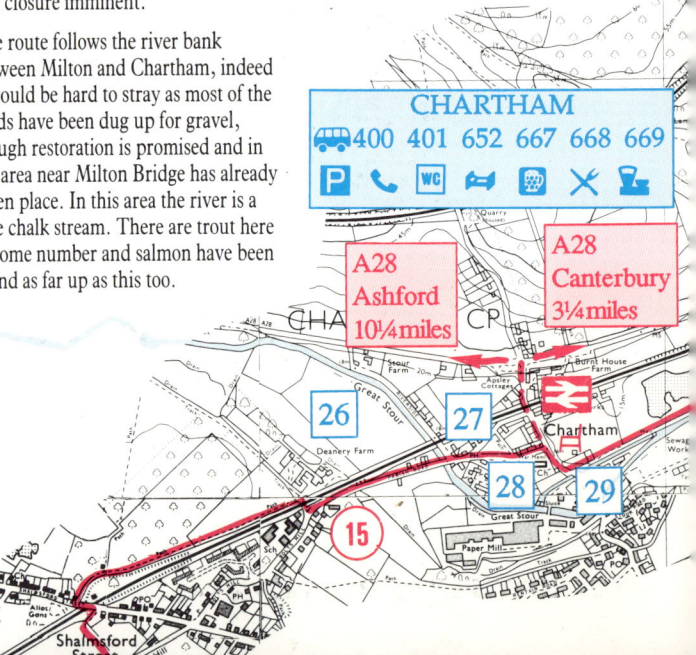

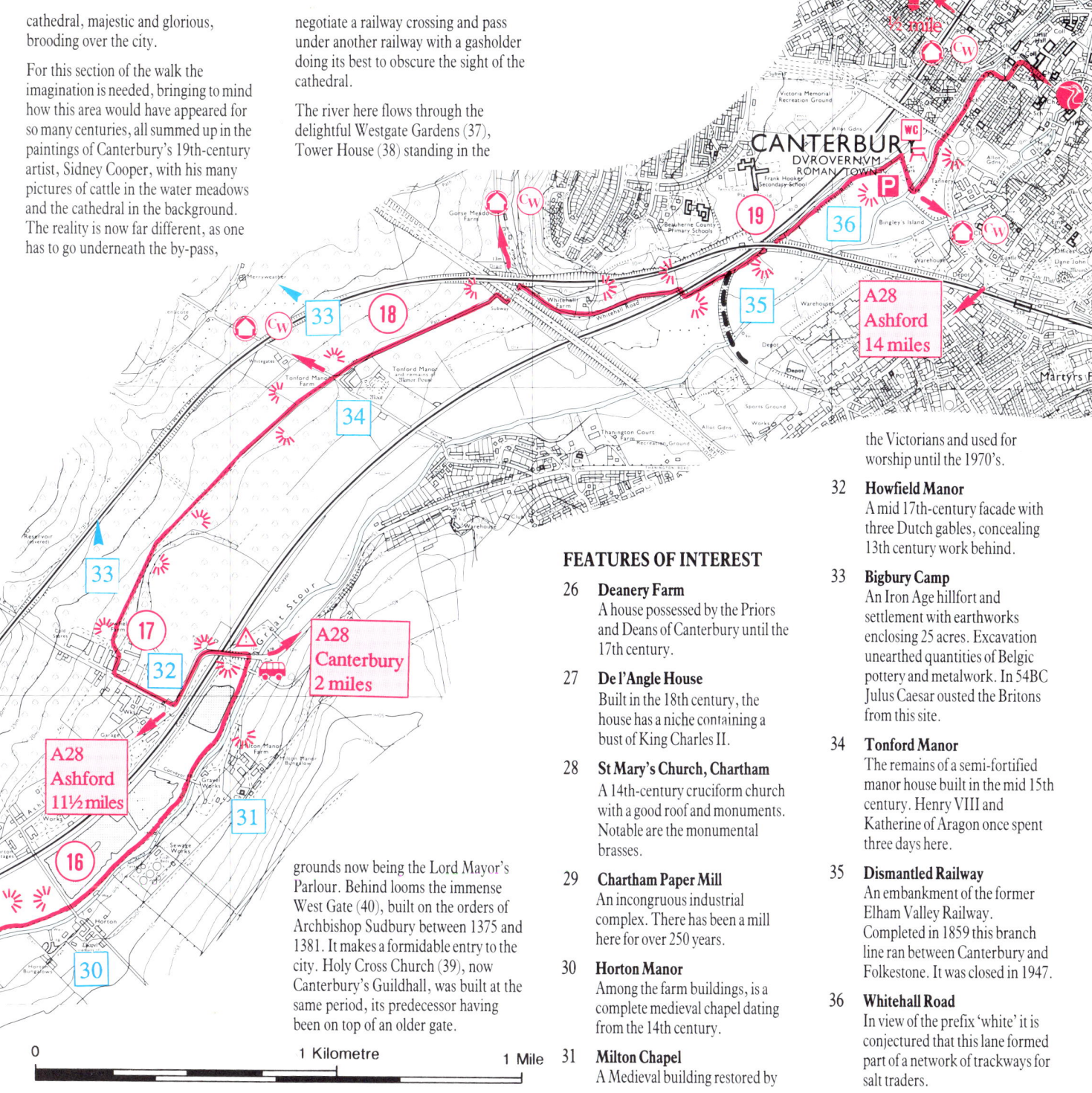

cathedral, majestic and glorious, brooding over the city.

For this section of the walk the imagination is needed, bringing to mind how this area would have appeared for so many centuries, all summed up in the paintings of Canterbury's 19th-century artist, Sidney Cooper, with his many pictures of cattle in the water meadows and the cathedral in the background. The reality is now far different, as one has to go underneath the by-pass, negotiate a railway crossing and pass under another railway with a gasholder doing its best to obscure the sight of the cathedral.

The river here flows through the delightful Westgate Gardens (37), Tower House (38) standing in the grounds now being the Lord Mayor's Parlour. Behind looms the immense West Gate (40), built on the orders of Archbishop Sudbury between 1375 and 1381. It makes a formidable entry to the city. Holy Cross Church (39), now Canterbury's Guildhall, was built at the same period, its predecessor having been on top of an older gate.

FEATURES OF INTEREST

26 Deanery Farm
A house possessed by the Priors and Deans of Canterbury until the 17th century.

27 De l'Angle House
Built in the 18th century, the house has a niche containing a bust of King Charles II.

28 St Mary's Church, Chartham
A 14th-century cruciform church with a good roof and monuments. Notable are the monumental brasses.

29 Chartham Paper Mill
An incongruous industrial complex. There has been a mill here for over 250 years.

30 Horton Manor
Among the farm buildings, is a complete medieval chapel dating from the 14th century.

31 Milton Chapel
A Medieval building restored by the Victorians and used for worship until the 1970's.

32 Howfield Manor
A mid 17th-century facade with three Dutch gables, concealing 13th century work behind.

33 Bigbury Camp
An Iron Age hillfort and settlement with earthworks enclosing 25 acres. Excavation unearthed quantities of Belgic pottery and metalwork. In 54BC Julius Caesar ousted the Britons from this site.

34 Tonford Manor
The remains of a semi-fortified manor house built in the mid 15th century. Henry VIII and Katherine of Aragon once spent three days here.

35 Dismantled Railway
An embankment of the former Elham Valley Railway. Completed in 1859 this branch line ran between Canterbury and Folkestone. It was closed in 1947.

36 Whitehall Road
In view of the prefix 'white' it is conjectured that this lane formed part of a network of trackways for salt traders.

CANTERBURY

FEATURES OF INTEREST

37 Westgate Gardens
The owners of Tower House landscaped and developed the site. In 1936 the house and garden were given to the city, the latter to become a public open space.

38 Tower House
Now the Lord Mayor's parlour, Tower House was once the home of the Williamson family who owned St Mildred's Tannery.

39 Church of the Holy Cross
Holy Cross Church was originally situated over an earlier West Gate, but was rebuilt on its present site by Archbishop Sudbury in 1380 when the new West Gate was built. It now serves as Canterbury's Guildhall.

41 St Dunstan's Church (¼ mile)
With fragments of the 11th century flint masonry, St Dunstan's Church is mainly work of the 14th and 15th centuries. Beneath St Nicholas' Chapel, in a vault, lies the head of Sir Thomas More, the Lord Chancellor of England who was beheaded by order of Henry VIII in 1535.

42 Roper Gateway (400 yards)
An elaborate Tudor red-brick structure which once led to the mansion of the Roper family. It was the home of Sir Thomas More's daughter, Margaret Roper, who brought her father's head to St Dunstans Church after his execution.

43 Sidney Cooper Cottage
The 15th century cottage was the birthplace of Sidney Cooper, the well-known Victorian painter. He established an art school in the building around his mother's cottage. It later became Canterbury College of Art until being re-sited adjacent to the College of Technology.

44 St Peter's (Methodist) Church
Set back from the street frontage is the Methodist Church, a finely proportioned classical revival building dating from 1811.

45 St Peter's (Anglican) Church
Dating from the Norman period, the interior of this unspoilt church has kept its medieval flavour. There is a fine Norman font and 17th-century sounding board (above the pulpit).

46 Greyfriars
The 1267 dormitory building which spans the river is all that remains of an extensive monastery. The Friary was demolished in 1538 at the time of the Dissolution.

47 Eastbridge Hospital
The Hospital was founded in 1180 by William Fitz Odbold as a hostel to care for the infirm and shelter poor pilgrims. After the reformation of 1538 it became an almshouse.

Christ Church Cathedral, Canterbury

St Augustine's Abbey ruins, Canterbury

48 'Weavers'
The house was originally a Kentish Hall House of the 12th century with later extensions in the 16th century. The house was the home and work-place of the Huguenots who fled the religious persecution of their own countries and set up a weaving industry in the city.

49 Blackfriars
The guest house and refectory (dining room) are the remaining buildings of the Blackfriars Priory founded c1236. In both buildings are preserved fine medieval timber roofs.

50 Abbots Mill
There were mills on this site for 800 years until 1933 when the latest mill, designed by John Smeaton, was burnt down. The mill race remains and the sluices and some machinery still exist.

51 St Mildred's Church
The church is built in the gothic style with parts of the nave dating back to the 8th century. Mildred was the great great granddaughter of King Ethelbert. Isaac Walton was married here in 1626.

52 Maynard and Cotton's Almshouses
An almshouse founded by a rich merchant, Maynard, who was licensed to coin money in the 12th century. Cotton, a wealthy pewterer enlarged the foundation in the 17th century. The present buildings date from 1708.

53 Poor Priest's Hospital
Founded in the 12th century by Archdeacon Simon Langton, this hospital was an almshouse for elderly and infirm clergy. The present buildings were erected in 1373. Now restored, it houses the Canterbury Heritage Museum.

54 Beaney Institute
The Beaney Institute, named after its benefactor, was opened in 1899. This Victorian building houses the city library and the Royal Museum and Art Gallery. There are, amongst other things, galleries for the paintings of Sidney Cooper and for the Buffs Regiment.

55 St Alphege Church
The present church was built soon after Archbishop Lanfranc realigned Palace Street to make way for his new palace opposite. It is used today as the Canterbury Urban Studies Centre.

56 Conquest House
Conquest House has a 17th century half-timbered front with a 12th century crypt where, traditionally, the four knights

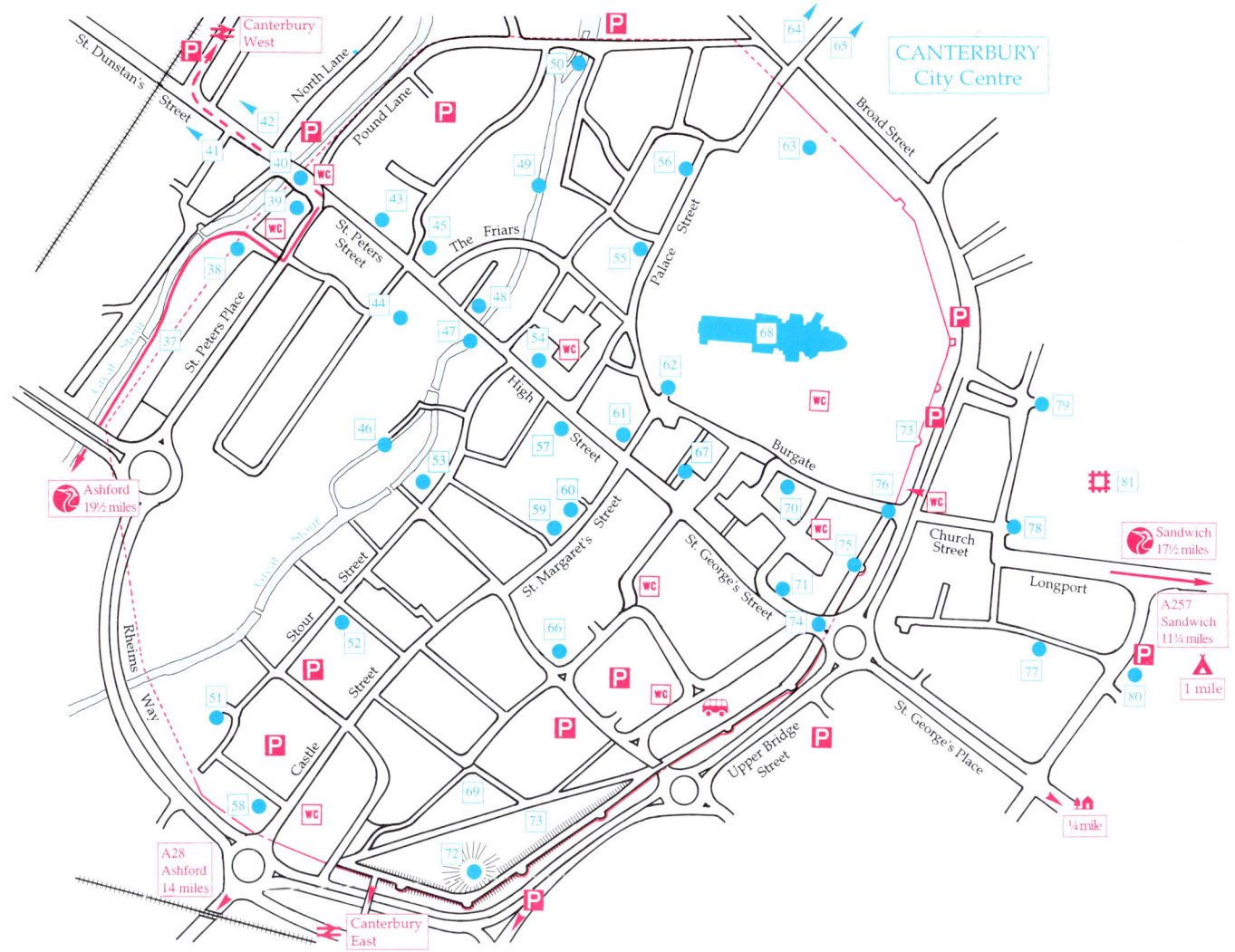

plotted to murder Thomas Becket. The front room, now a shop, has a coat of arms of Charles I above the fireplace.

57 Queen Elizabeth's Guest Chamber
This half-timbered structure is of Elizabethan date, its finest feature being the pargeting (ornamental plaster moulding) on the front. Queen Elizabeth I entertained the Duc d'Alecon during her 1573 visit.

58 Castle Keep
The keep is all that remains of the Norman Castle which was built soon after the Conquest. The keep is the fifth largest of its kind in the country; it originally had three stories, but now reduced in height. It served as a county jail for years, then later a coal store.

59 Visitor Information Centre

60 St Margaret's Church
This redundant medieval church with extensive restoration work by Sir Gilbert Scott now houses 'The Canterbury Tales' which provides fascinating glimpses into the tales and adventures of Chaucer's pilgrims on their way to worship at the Shrine of Thomas Becket.

The Stour Valley walk is not signposted through Canterbury. You are, therefore, given the opportunity of devising your own route through the centre of this historic city, to visit the many places and features of interest.

The route is signed and waymarked westwards from the West Gate, and eastwards from St Augustine's Abbey.

61 **'Chequers of the Hope'**
This inn was built by Prior Chillenden in the late 1390's to provide rest and refreshment for medieval pilgrims. The stone arches on the ground floor of the shop are all that remain of the hostelry burnt down in 1860.

62 **Christ Church Gateway**
The gateway is an example of Perpendicular architecture built by Prior Goldstone between 1502 and 1519. The turrets having been removed in the 18th century were restored between 1937 and 1939.

63 **Norman Staircase (King's School)**
The King's School now occupying the the ancient building of the Christ Church Monastery and one of the oldest scholastic foundations in England, is noted for its fine exterior Norman Staircase.

64 **Hospital of St John the Baptist (300 yards)**
This hospital, now an almshouse, located in Northgate, was originally founded in 1084 by Archbishop Lanfranc.

65 **Jesus Hospital (⅓ mile)**
Another almshouse further along Northgate, is Jesus Hospital, built in 1590 and enlarged in 1935.

66 **16 Watling Street**
A town house built in the early 17th century, which survived the bombing in World War II.

67 **Roman Pavement**
In Butchery Lane, underground, is preserved the remains of a Roman town house unearthed after the blitz of World War II with its hypocaust room (heating system) and mosaic pavement. It is closed, temporarily, during excavation work.

68 **Christ Church Cathedral**
Christ Church Cathedral was built on the site of an earlier church

Canterbury Castle

destroyed by fire in 1067. It was started by Lanfranc in 1070 and added to in all building styles through to Perpendicular. The principal features are the Norman crypt, the site of Thomas Becket's shrine, the tombs of Henry IV and Edward the Black Prince, the 12th century choir and 14th century screen.

69 **Dane John Gardens**
The gardens were laid out and presented to the city by Alderman James Simmons in 1790. In the centre is a memorial to Christopher Marlowe in the form of a muse. His memory is kept alive in the modern Marlowe Theatre in The Friars.

70 **St Mary Magdalene's Church Tower**
The isolated tower of a church which was demolished in 1871. The tower was built in 1502 in the Perpendicular style of the period.

71 **St George's Church Tower**
Following the bombing raids during the last war, the sole survivor in this area of the city is the tower of St George's Church, where Marlowe, one of Canterbury's famous authors, was baptised in 1564.

72 **Dane John**
Originally a bronze age burial mound, the present shape of Dane John (derived from the name Donjon) dates back only to 1790 when Alderman Simmons transformed an earlier defensive mound into a feature for the gardens.

73 **City Wall**
Long streches of the Roman walls, as rebuilt in the 14th and 15th centuries, remain. The walls are built of flint and the southernmost section is accompanied by its original ditch.

74 **St George's Gate (site of)**
The gateway, which was rebuilt in 1470 (recent excavations revealed that it was similar in shape to West Gate), served as a defendable entry point to the city. The gateway was demolished in 1801.

75 **Zoar Chapel**
The city wall bastion was used as a water tower in the early 19th century. The Zoar Chapel was established by the Zoar Baptists in 1845.

76 **Burgate (site of)**
The 'Bur' 'Bar' or 'Borough' Gate, rebuilt of brick in 1475, stood at the entrance to Burgate. Most of the gateway was demolished in 1781, the remaining tower in 1822.

77 **Old Hall**
The most notable building in Ivy Lane is a late 14th-century timber-framed house known as Old Hall. It is a typical Wealden-type hall house.

78 **Cemetry Gate**
Now used as a house, Cemetry Gate was one of the gateways to St Augustine's Abbey. It was built before 1391 and restored in 1839.

79 **St Augustine's Gate**
The great gateway of St Augustine's Abbey, or Fyndon Gate was built in 1301-9. The style of the period is Decorated with hints of Perpendicular. It was restored after bomb damage.

80 **T S and H Cooper Almshouses**
These almshouses were built in Victorian times and the style reflects the flemish influence of an earlier period.

81 **St Augustine's Abbey**
These ruins are extensive remains of a medieval Benedictine abbey overlying ruins of earlier 7th and 11th century abbeys. Founded in 598 by St Augustine, it includes the abbey church, cloisters and St Pancras Church.

Detail of south-west door, Canterbury Cathedral